Quentin Blake

A JERWOOD GALLERY NOTEBOOK

Walter Sickert

The beaches that Walter Sickert knew best were probably at Dieppe. He was a frequent visitor, as were Degas (whom he knew well) and other painters of the time. St Rémy, the church in the Jerwood painting, is in Dieppe. Sickert had a long and productive life as a painter; he lived and worked in London, where at one time and another he had several studios, as well as painting in France and in Venice. His collected journalism is also fascinating, almost like listening to the live conversations of a painter of a hundred years ago.

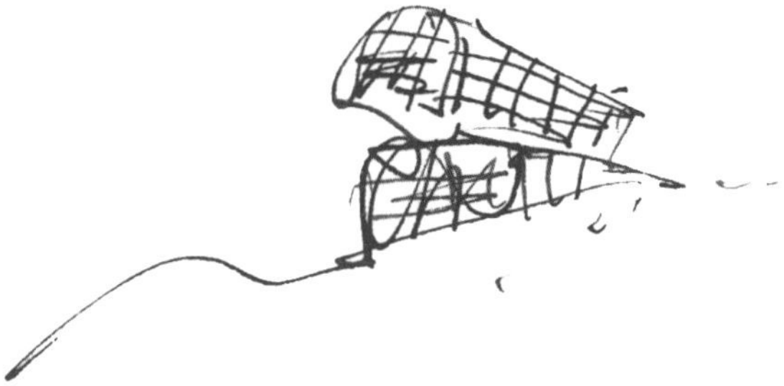

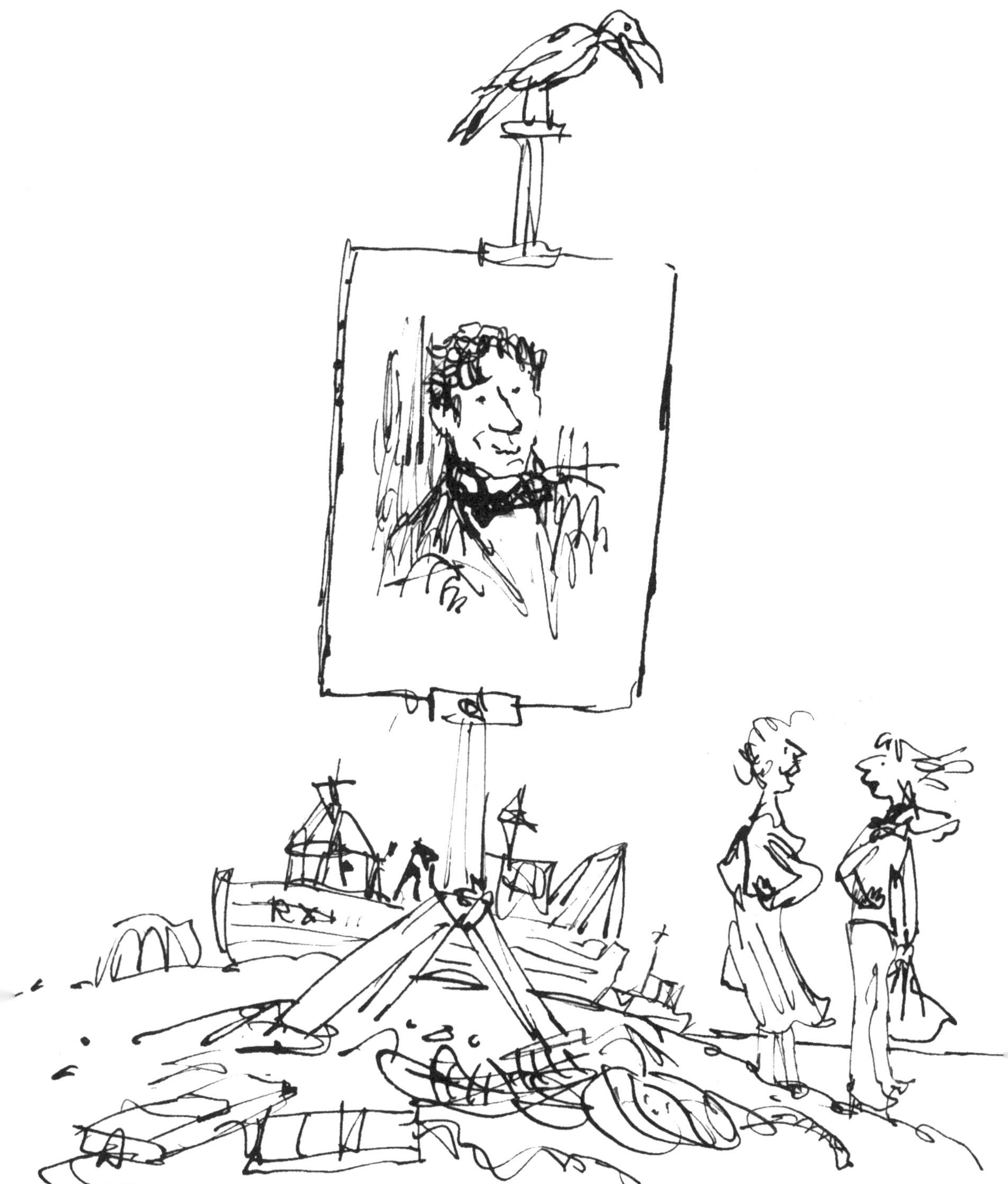

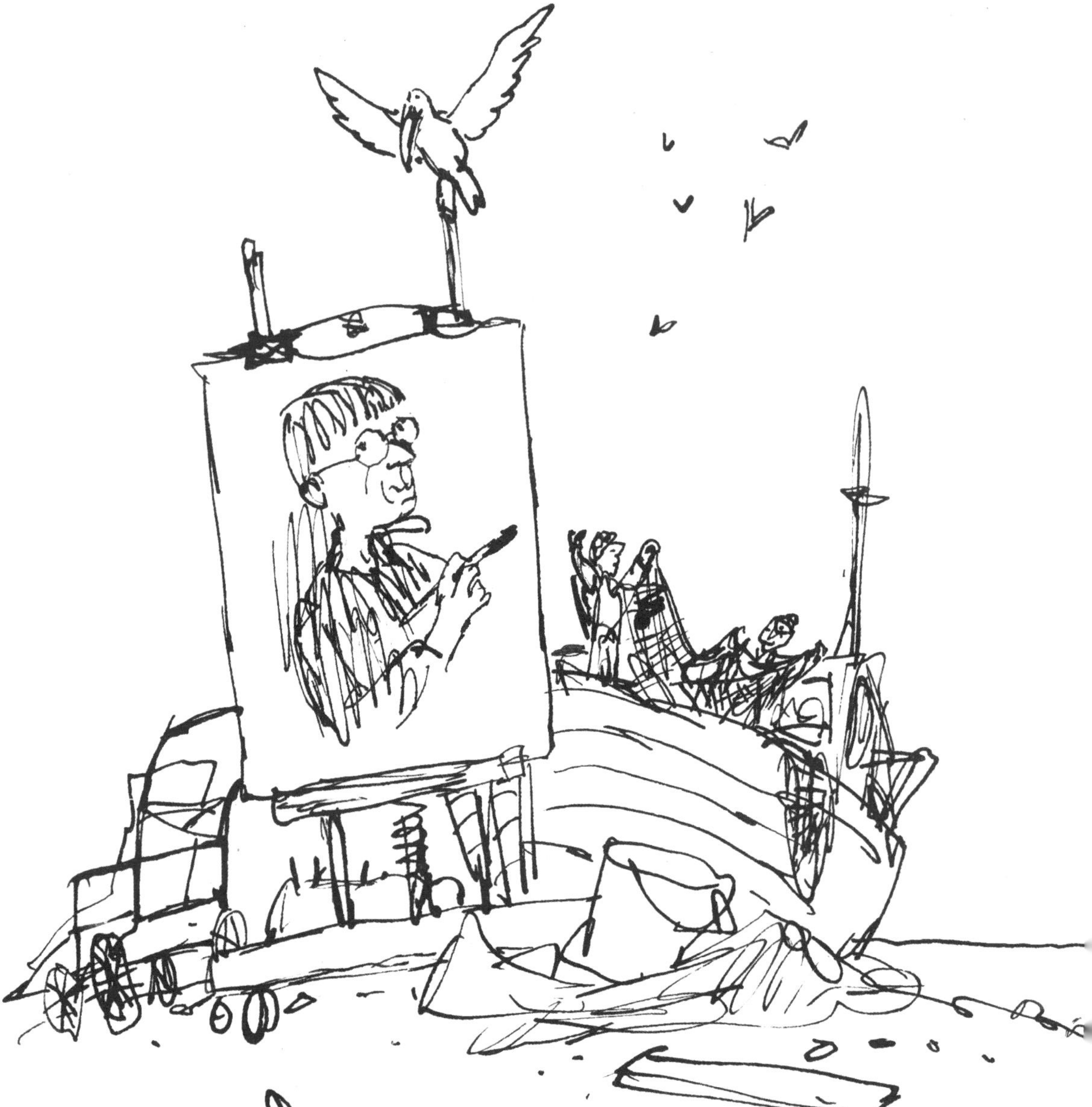

Stanley Spencer

Stanley Spencer is known as a visionary painter, celebrated for his paintings of mainly Biblical subjects, which all take place in his own native village of Cookham in Berkshire. His work in the Jerwood Collection is a remarkable portrait of Daphne Spencer, the artist's niece. It isn't just naturalistic; somehow its organisation and the intensity of its detail make it really memorable. When Spencer went out painting he often took with him a pram for his materials which had a notice on it 'Please do not talk to the artist while he is at work'. Though I don't expect Spencer ever got to Hastings beach, I couldn't resist drawing it in.

Alfred Wallis

Alfred Wallis was a Cornish mariner and fisherman. He took up painting for company after his wife had died and he had retired from work. Wallis would work on any odd piece of card that came to hand, often using ship's paint to create his pictures. He had no formal education, but developed his own artistic language to capture his memories and experience of the sea. His works have idiosyncratic qualities of colour, design and spontaneity that were very much admired by Ben Nicholson, who bought many of his paintings, and by other painters who lived in St Ives.

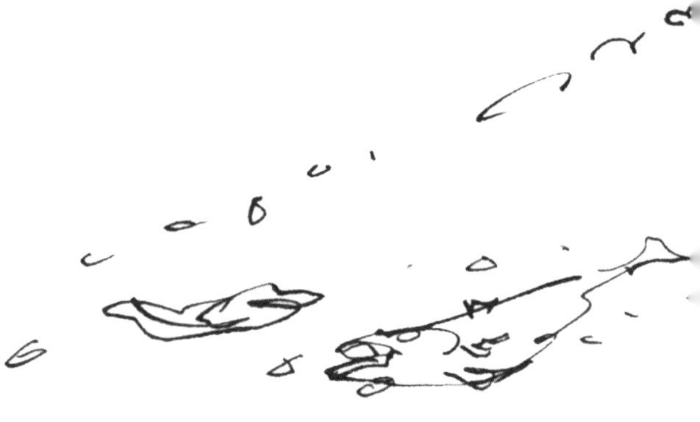

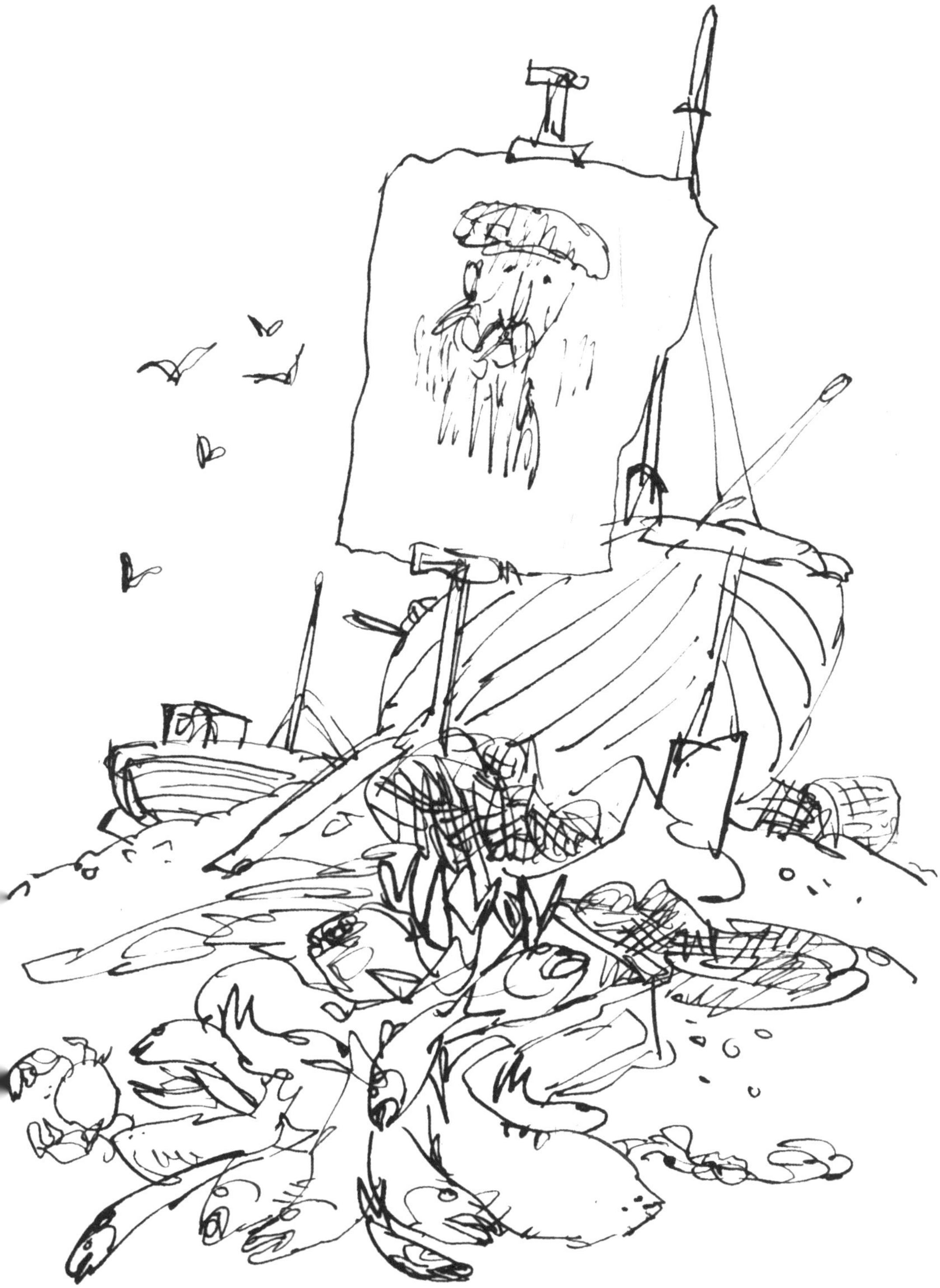

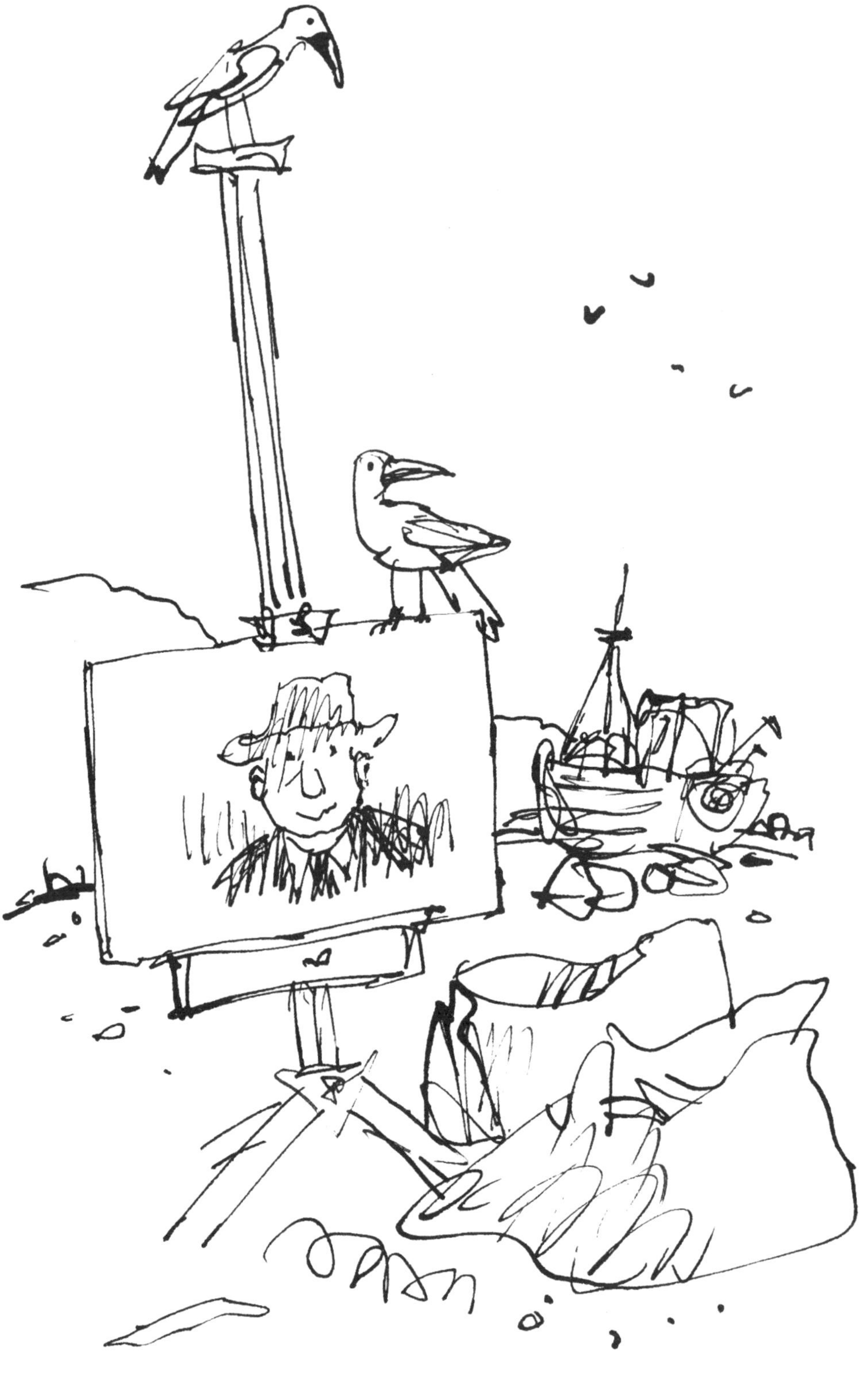

L.S. Lowry

Beaches seem a long way from L.S. Lowry's favourite industrial and urban landscapes. The Jerwood picture is of the top lock at Fairfield on the Aston Canal (a junction between Manchester and Ashton-under-Lyne). It was a typical local subject for Lowry, who believed you should always paint the place you know. His paintings seem to make no acknowledgement of other contemporary artistic styles, and though they are determinedly realistic, (who else would have put that tall chimney so centrally in the picture?) there still seems to me to be some sense of dream and nostalgia about them.

Prunella Clough

Prunella Clough was born in London and studied at both Chelsea and Wimbledon Schools of Art. She was teaching in Chelsea when I went there as a part-time student in the 1950's; she was known for her pictures of the fishermen of Southwold and industrial dockside activity on the Thames, and I can remember being impressed by their remarkable combination of taste, strength and design. I like to think she would have appreciated the sense of working life on Hastings Fishing Beach, and perhaps especially the tractors.

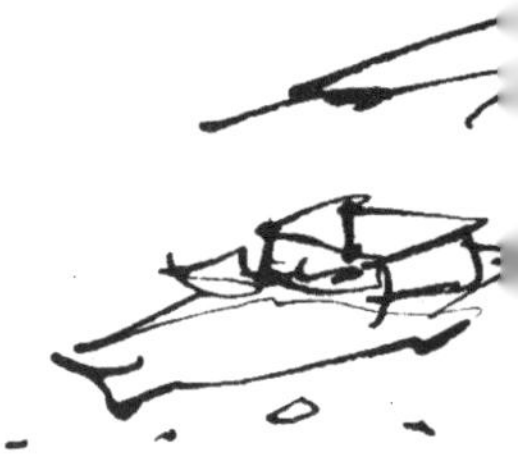

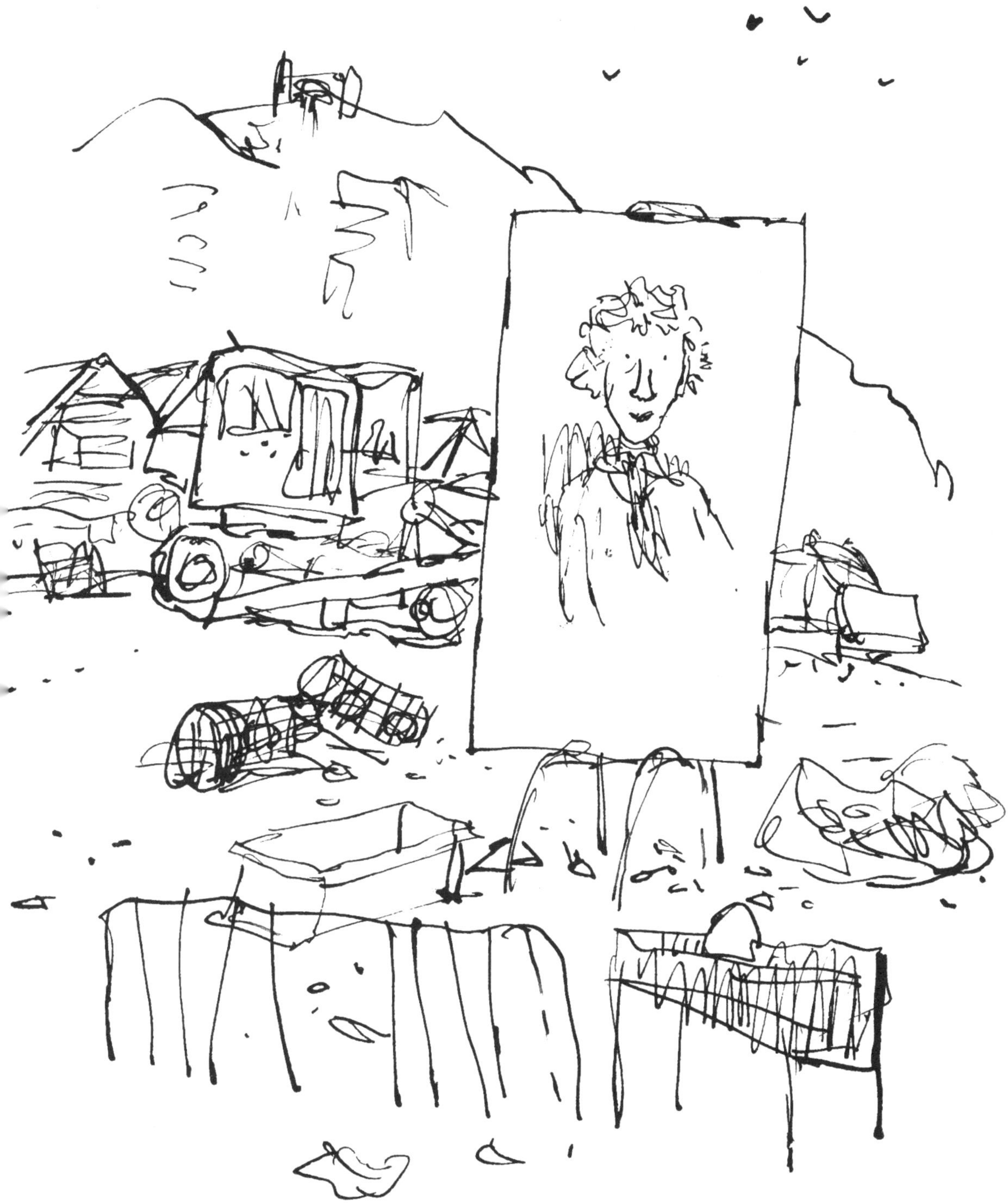

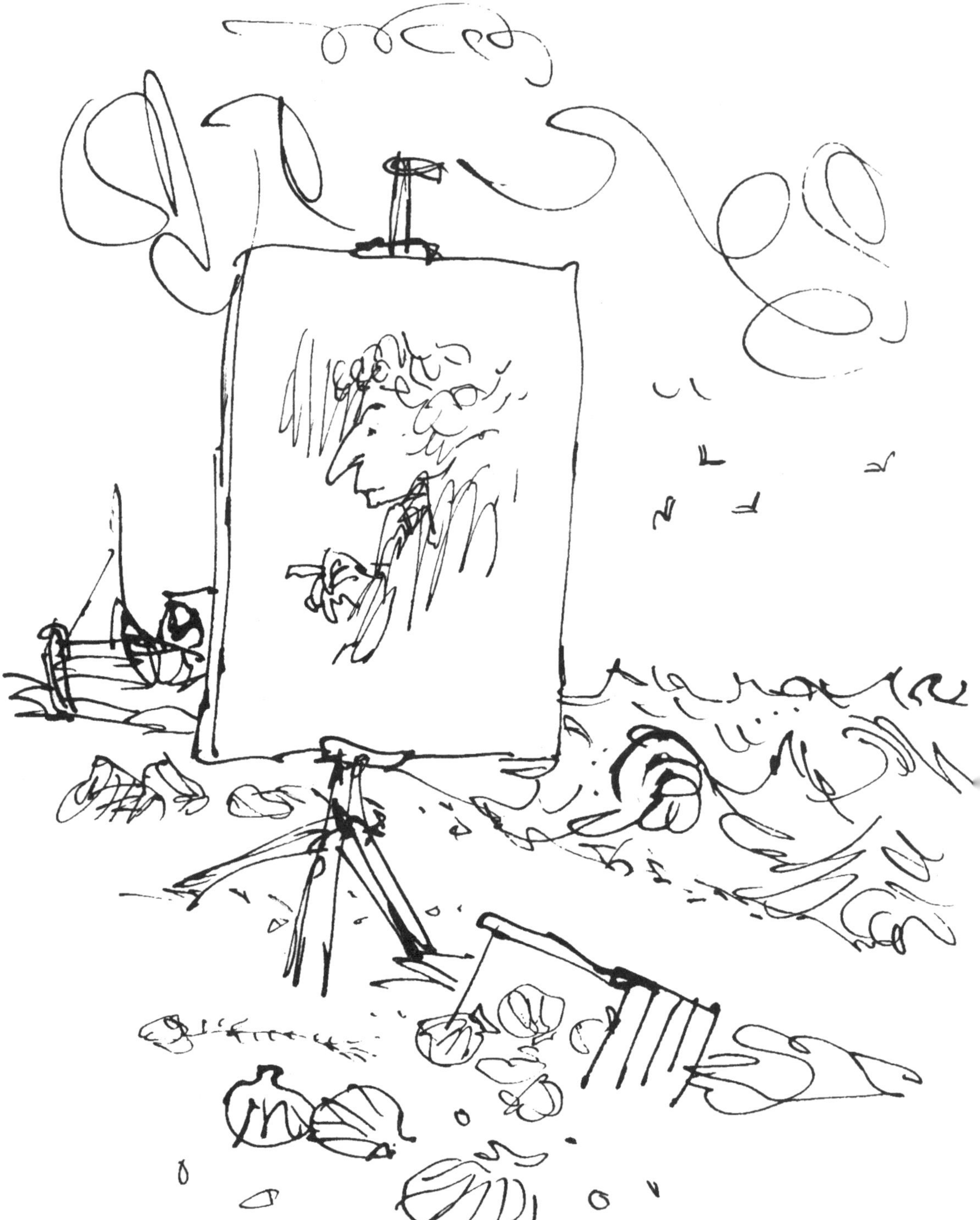

Maggi Hambling

Maggi Hambling was present on Hastings beach for the start of building work on the Jerwood Gallery, operating a bulldozer to perform the first ground-breaking. The beaches she is most likely to find herself on are in East Anglia, and Hambling has painted many canvasses simply of waves in motion inspired by the sea. Hambling won the second Jerwood Painting Prize in 1995. The portrait in the Jerwood Collection is of Frances Rose, a former neighbour, who, despite severe arthritis in her hands was still active in her 80s, washing and sewing for others.

Dod Procter

I am grateful to the Jerwood Gallery for introducing me to the work of an artist whom I didn't know till now except by name. Dod Procter gained international acclaim in her own lifetime with portraits such as the one of Lilian in the Jerwood collection, which manages to be formal, strong and intimate at the same time. Lilian was probably one of the local girls in Newlyn in Cornwall, where Dod Procter lived with her husband and fellow artist, Ernest.

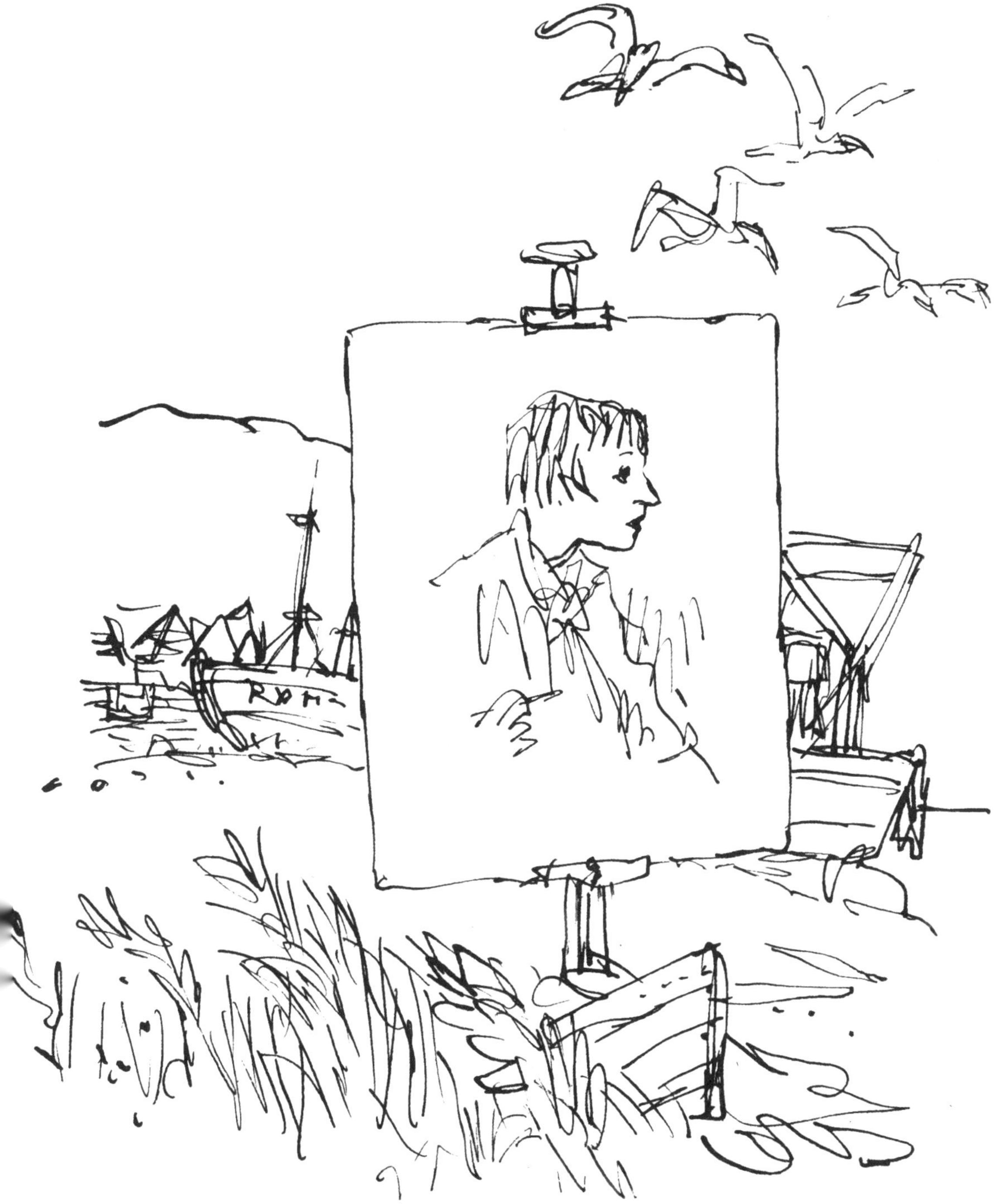

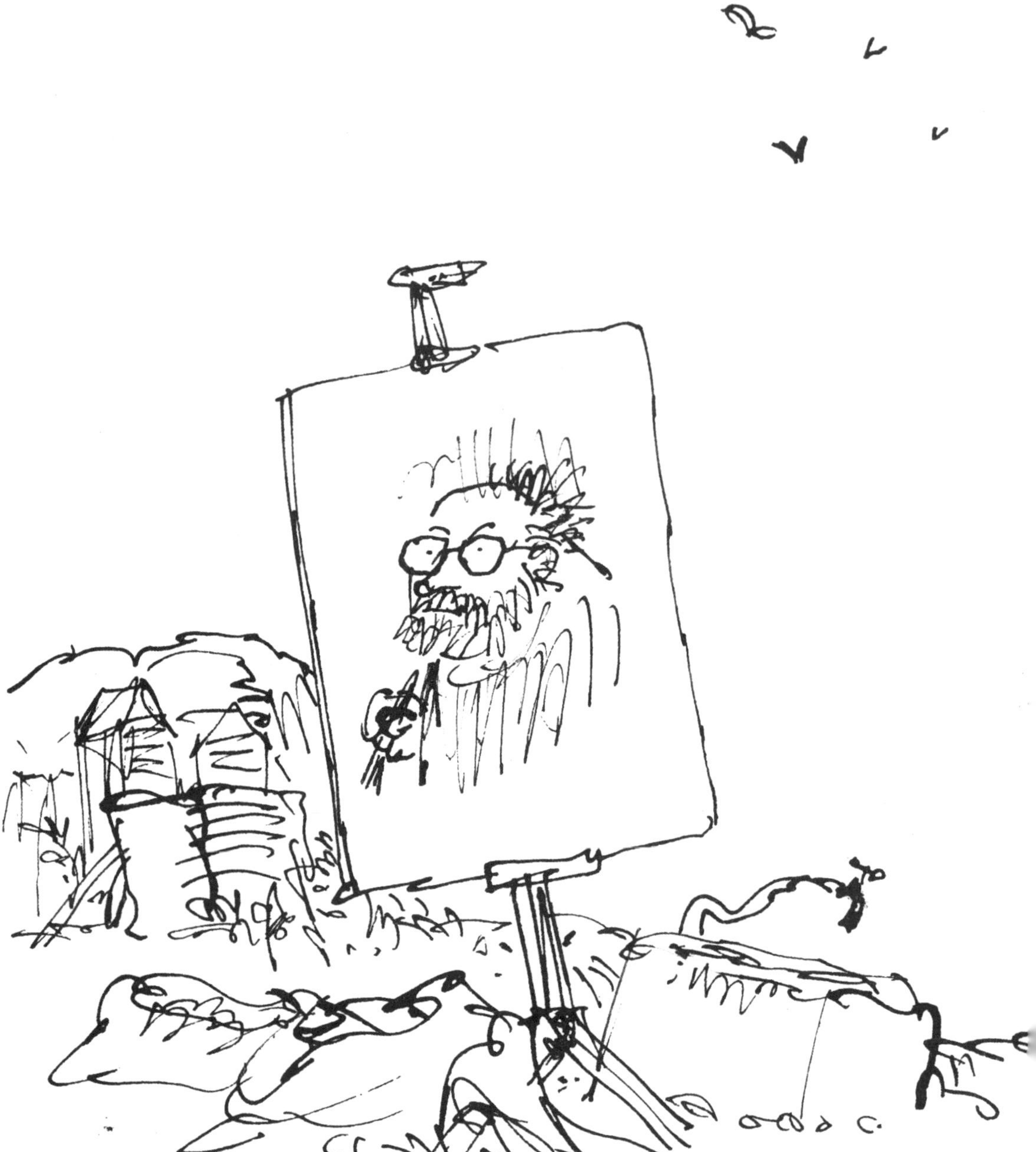

John Bratby

John Bratby came to prominence in the 1950s as one of a group of painters known as The Kitchen Sink School. It wasn't a name they chose themselves, but nevertheless a characteristic painting of the time might have been a portrait of the artist himself or of his wife, the artist Jean Cooke, with a table top cluttered with tins and packets and other kitchen items. One can't help but notice that the melon in the Jerwood painting has its label on show. Bratby lived in Hastings from the late-1970s until his death in 1992, in the Cupola, a house on Belmont Hill with wonderful views over the town.

Christopher Wood

Christopher (Kit) Wood died tragically at the age of 29; nevertheless through the 20s and 30s he had created a body of work distinctively his own and of its time. He was in contact with Ben Nicholson and his circle at St Ives, had lived in Paris, where he made the acquaintance of Picasso, and made many paintings of boats and fishing villages in Brittany. We don't know whether the beach shown in the Jerwood picture is in Cornwall or France. Although an ostensibly cheerful subject, it's perhaps possible to detect some sense of foreboding about it.

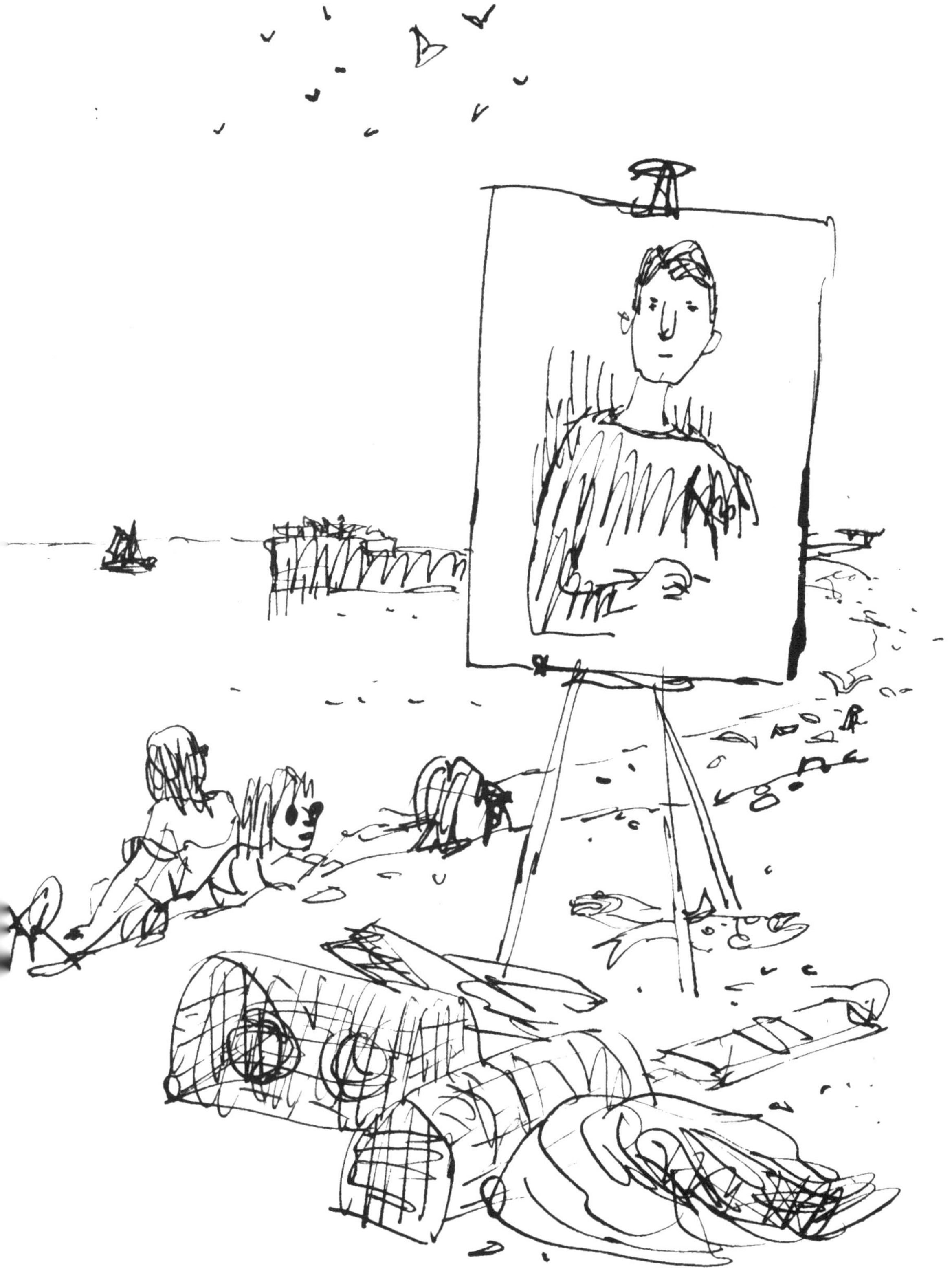

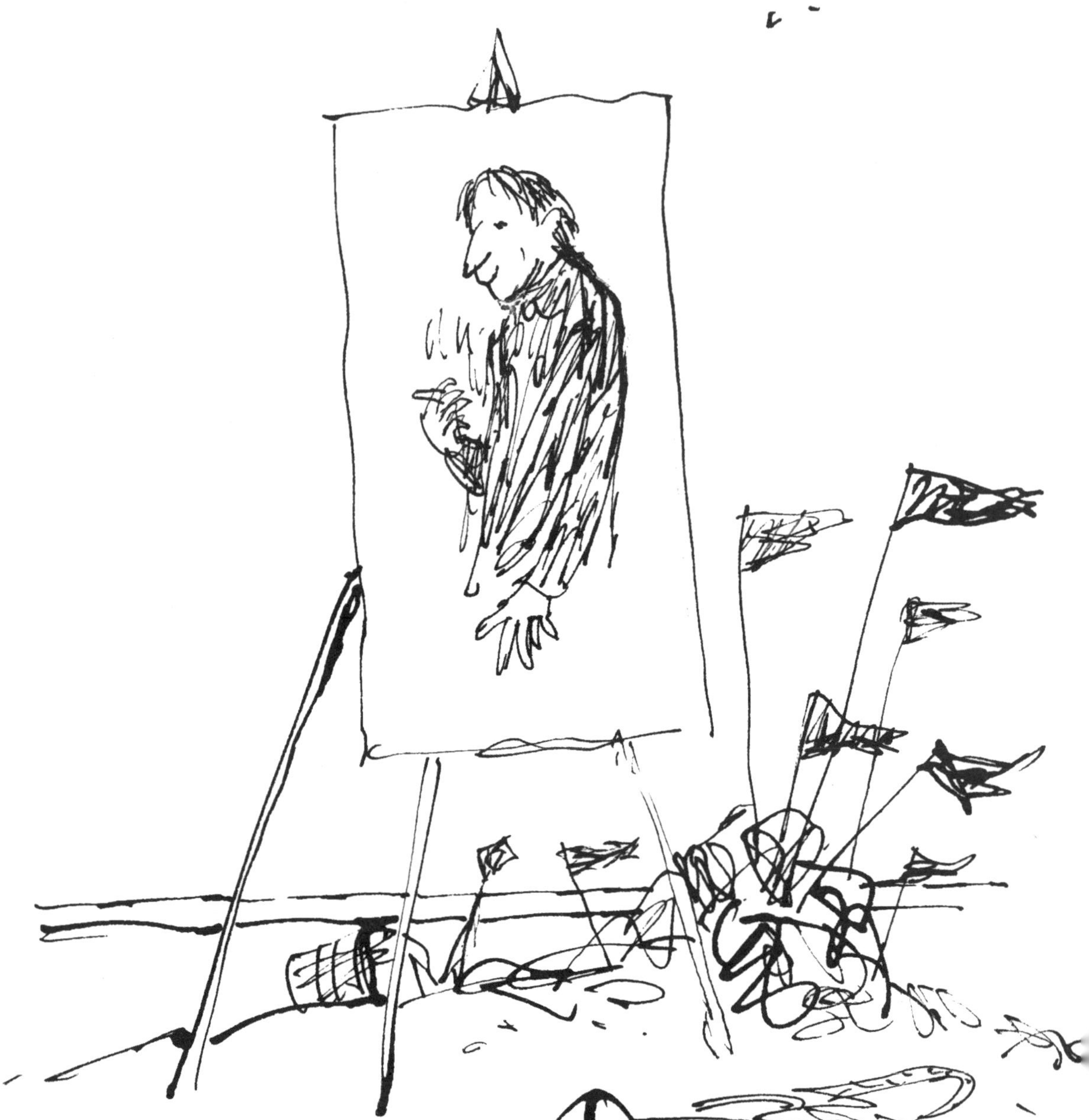

Edward Burra

Edward Burra was a local artist who was born and lived much of his life in Rye, and died in Hastings. Nevertheless he travelled widely and his earlier works take a satirical look at characters and situations he encountered in places such as Berlin and Harlem. In fact they are in style, it seems to me, more continental than English. The ghostly figures and foreboding sky in Burra's painting of Rye churchyard give it a mysterious and disturbing feel. Curiously for a picture so large, it's painted in watercolour. Burra's arthritis prevented him from using oil paints – but his detailed and subtle way of using watercolour (quite unlike the English watercolour landscape tradition) seems to suit him perfectly.

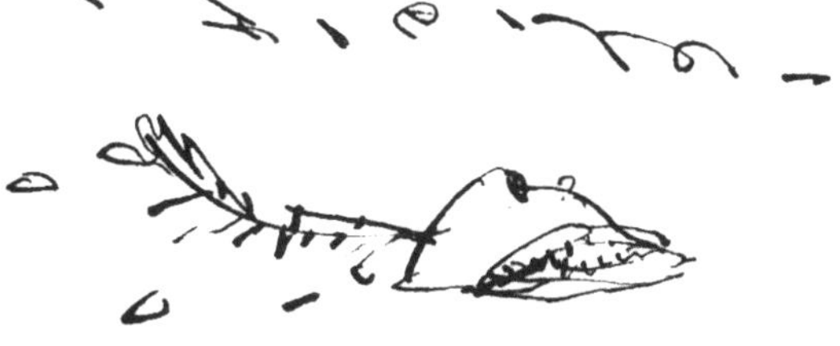

Production by Graham Rees Design
Printed by The Five Castles Press Ltd

Published by Jerwood Gallery, Hastings, 2014
ISBN 978-0-9571892-5-6

JERWOOD GALLERY

Rock-a-Nore Road
Hastings
East Sussex
TN34 3DW
Tel: + 44 (0)1424 728377
Email: info@jerwoodgallery.org
Web: www.jerwoodgallery.org